Emotional Intelligence 2.0

To live a better life, achieve success at work and happier relationships, improve your social skills, emotional agility, manage and influence people

Joseph Griffith

©Copyright 2020 Joseph Griffith All rights reserved

The content within this book may not be reproduced, duplicated, or transmitted without direct written permission from the author or the publisher.

Under no circumstances will any blame or legal responsibility be held against the publisher, or author, for any damages, reparation, or monetary loss due to the information contained within this book, either directly or indirectly.

Legal Notice

This book is copyright protected. This book is only for personal use. You cannot amend, distribute, sell, use, quote, or paraphrase any part, or the content within this book, without the consent of the author-publisher.

Disclaimer Notice

Please note that the information contained within this document is for educational and entertainment purposes only. All effort has been executed to present accurate, up-to-date, and reliable, complete information. No warranties of any kind are declared or implied. Readers acknowledge that the author is not engaging in the rendering of legal, financial, medical, or professional advice.

TABLE OF CONTENTS

Book Description 4

Introduction 6

Chapter 1: What is Emotional Intelligence, and Why is it Important? 14

Chapter 2: The Four Attributes of Emotional Intelligence 27

Chapter 3: Busting Myths About Emotional Intelligence. 54

Chapter 4: Steps on How to Grow Emotional Intelligence 63

Chapter 5: Emotional Intelligence at School/Workplace 75

Chapter 6: Emotional Intelligence and Health 82

Chapter 7: Emotional Intelligence and Relationships 90

Chapter 8: The Interaction Between EQ and Social Intelligence 102

Chapter 9: Understanding Emotional Drain and Dealing with Them 116

One Last Word 122

Book Description

Do you feel like you have been stuck in the same place for so long without making progress? Do you feel like the decisions you have been making lately are all over the place? Do you want to build stronger relationships, succeed at work and in school? Do you wish to achieve your career and personal growth? Do you consider yourself with emotional intelligence? If not, then rest assured that you have come to the right place!

One thing that is important to bear in mind is that Emotional Intelligence plays a significant role in helping you recognize, manage, and understand your emotions and how they influence those of others. It is through emotional intelligence that you can boost your performance – whether in your personal life, at home, or in the workplace.

Think of a place where your confidence, optimism, empathy, self-control, and social skills all work hand in hand to accelerate success in all areas of your life. Do you want that?

In this book, you will learn:

- What Emotional Intelligence is
- The keys to Emotional intelligence
- How you can identify your emotions and those of others
- How to use your feelings to guide your thinking and reasoning
- To understand how feelings change and develop with the unfolding of events
- To manage to open your arms to feeling data and using that to make informed choices for success

So, what are you still waiting for?

It is time to sharpen your intuitions and position yourself for success and a better life.

Come with me!

Introduction

You have probably heard of emotional intelligence at home, school, or in the workplace. This concept continues to grow in popularity, especially in a brain-dead world where people strive to achieve success but don't know how to connect with their emotional feelings to realize their goals.

You may be thinking, "Why is emotional intelligence growing in importance among peers in an evolving workplace or in life in general?"

One thing that is important to bear in mind is that emotional intelligence is not a trend. It is here to stay. According to reports and statistics compiled by major companies across the world, it is evident that people's emotional intelligence affect their bottom line. For instance, if an employee has a high level of emotional intelligence, they will not only be productive and generate revenue for the company, but they will also achieve their personal and career goals.

Look around you. Are there people you know, whether at home or the workplace, with high emotional intelligence? Do you know people who are really good listeners? They can communicate well in a variety of circumstances. It is almost like they know exactly what to say, when to say it, and how to say it, so that others are not offended. These people are caring, considerate, and can find solutions for problems. When you approach them for guidance, they leave you feeling optimistic and more hopeful in life.

You probably know other people who have mastered the art of managing their emotions. Instead of getting angry when provoked by a stressful situation, they choose to look at the problem from a different perspective to calmly find a solution. These people are excellent decision-makers and have mastered the art of listening to their gut feeling. Regardless of their strengths, they have the willingness to look at themselves with an honest eye. They take criticism positively and use it to improve their performance.

It is this kind of person that we wish to emulate.

What sets them apart is a high degree of emotional intelligence. You can have that too. You can learn how to manage your emotions in every situation, while ensuring that you take care of the emotional needs of the people around you.

You may be thinking, "I can never be like this. I don't have what it takes to be like these people."

I am here to tell you that you can be just like these people. As you begin to implement emotional intelligence into your life, you will begin to see an improvement in your technical abilities, interrelationships, and overall success. It is through emotional intelligence that you can improve your performance. It impacts your confidence, optimism, self-control, empathy and social skills, so that you can understand and manage your emotions and accelerate success in every area of your life.

It does not matter what your profession is, whether you work for a small or a large organization, whether you are a senior or junior in your company. What matters is that realizing how effective you are at controlling your emotional energies is the beginning of a successful adventure. Emotional intelligence may not be something taught and tested in many educational curricula, but it is really important.

The good news is that it is something you and I can learn, which is why we have compiled a book with all the tips that will help you improve your emotional intelligence skills and implement them in everyday life. Our clients have given us positive feedback on how these skills have not only helped them advance in life but have also helped them motivate and inspire others to be better.

In summary, emotional intelligence is what helps you identify your emotions, manage them effectively, and constructively react to others' emotions. When you understand how those emotions shape your thoughts and actions, you gain better control of your behavior and establish a new skill set that will help you to effectively manage your emotions. When you are emotionally conscious, you position yourself for growth and a deeper understanding of who you truly are. This way, you can communicate better with people around you and can strengthen your relationships.

To get you started, you must discover the foundation of your emotional intelligence. The best way to do that is to observe your feelings.

Practice Observing Your Feelings

Take a look at your life. Chances are that you will notice how hectic and busy your lifestyle is. This kind of life makes it easy for you to lose touch with yourself and with your emotional feelings. You might consider trying to reconnect with your feelings by setting a timer for various points throughout the day. As soon as the timer goes off, stop what you are doing, stand on your two feet, and take in a deep breath. Bring your thoughts to what you are feeling in that moment, where the emotions are coming from, and where you feel the sensation in your body and what it feels like. The more you practice this, the more it will become your second nature.

Pay Attention to How You Act

As you practice self-awareness, pay attention to how you act and behave in different situations. When you experience a certain emotion, observe what your actions are like and how they affect your daily activities. You will realize that managing your feelings comes easily, and your reactions become more conscious.

Question Your Opinion

We all live in a hyper-connected world that makes it easy to fall into a "bubble of opinions." You find yourself in a state of existence where your opinions are reinforced by others all the time. The last thing you want is for your voice to be completely lost because you are always flowing with the urges of life and what others decide for you.

Take time to evaluate multiple sides of the story and bring your views forward with confidence. It does not matter what people think of you and your opinions. What matters most is that you are willing to get your opinions challenged even when you feel that you are right. This way, you gain a better understanding of others and become more receptive to their ideas.

Be Responsible for Your Emotional Feelings

The first thing about responsibility is accepting the fact that your emotions and actions come from you. It does not matter what the situation or circumstances are like, because no one tells you to react the way you do. No one tells you to feel what you feel. When you accept the responsibility for your feelings and actions, you begin to have a positive impact in your life.

Celebrate the Positives in Your Life

One key to emotional intelligence is to celebrate and reflect on all the positives in your life. No one has a perfect life; we all go through ups and downs. Whether you have more positives or negatives in your life, the trick to celebrate every victory – big or small. When you accept the positives in your life, you allow yourself to develop more resilience and you increase your chances of enjoying fulfilling relationships so that you can successfully move past adversity.

Don't Ignore the Negatives

Just because you have chosen to embrace and celebrate the positives in your life does not mean that you ignore the negatives. Take time to reflect on negative feelings you might have, just as you would the positive feelings. This will help you understand the root cause of these negative feelings so that you can master how to control them.

Breathe

No matter what life throws your way, it is essential to take time to just breathe. Taking time to take deep breaths will help you manage your emotions and avoid outbursts. Walk out the door and wash your face with cold water, take a walk, or just take in fresh air – anything to calm your nerves. This goes a long way in helping you get a hold of what is happening so that you can effectively respond to the situation.

That said, emotional intelligence is a lifetime process. It is not something you develop overnight. To grow your emotional intelligence you have to train your mind to accept continual improvements along the way, so that you can be better with each passing day.

Chapter 1:
What is Emotional Intelligence, and Why is it Important?

Most people don't know what emotional intelligence is, even though it is something we should have in our lives. Emotional intelligence simply refers to the ability to identify our emotional feelings and manage them, and those of people around us.

Emotional intelligence generally involves three key skills:

- Emotional awareness, which is the ability to identify your emotional feelings and name them
- The ability to connect with our emotional feelings and apply them into problem-solving, thinking and reasoning
- The ability to manage our emotional feelings, which includes regulating them where necessary and helping people around us to do the same

Unlike the general intelligence that has a psychometric test or scale, emotional intelligence does not have one. This is the reason some people think of emotional intelligence not as an actual construct but instead as an interpersonal skill. However, despite all the criticism, emotional intelligence is sometimes referred to as the emotional quotient (EQ).

Today, several companies have included emotional intelligence tests into their application and interview processes, mainly because they think a high emotional intelligence makes one a good coworker or leader.

While there are research studies that have demonstrated a link between emotional intelligence and job performance, there are others that show no correlation. The lack of a scientifically valid scale to measure emotional intelligence makes it challenging for one to accurately measure or predict one's emotional intelligence, whether at home or in the workplace.

So, what does it mean to be emotionally intelligent?

Someone who is emotionally intelligent is highly conscious of their emotional states, whether negative, such as sad or frustrated, or positive, such as happy and subtle. If you can identify your emotional feelings and manage them effectively, then chances are that you have emotional intelligence. For you to be called emotionally intelligent, demonstrate that you are tuned to the emotions other people are experiencing. When you can sense and understand what other people are going through, you become a better friend, parent, partner, or leader. The good thing is that you can hone these skills easily with the tips we will give you in this book.

When emotional intelligence was first introduced, it played a role in uniquely filling the missing link: people with average IQ outperform those with a high IQ. It is because of this anomaly that people amended their assumption that IQ was the only source of success.

Research studies point to emotional intelligence as a central factor in differentiating between high performers and the rest of the pack. This correlation is so strong that over 90% of the top performers are said to have high emotional intelligence.

In other words, emotional intelligence is the intangible thing each one of us has that influences how we behave, handle social complexities, and make decisions to achieve success.

Despite the significance EQ has on our lives, its intangible nature makes it hard for us to know how much of it we have and what it is that we can do to improve it if we lack it.

So, how can you tell when you have emotional intelligence?

Robust Emotional Vocabulary

We all experience emotional feelings of different kinds, but we don't handle them the same way. Many people cannot accurately identify their emotions as they happen. Research demonstrates that at least 36% of people can identify their emotions as soon as they occur. A large number of individuals are unable to label their emotional feelings – hence contributing to misunderstandings. This explains why people end up making irrational decisions and engaging in counterproductive behaviors.

When you have a high EQ, you will not only master your emotions but also understand them and use a sophisticated vocabulary to describe your feelings. While there are times when someone says that they feel "bad," emotional intelligence allows one to specifically pinpoint their emotions as irritable, demoralized, frustrated, or anxious. In other words, when your word choice is specific, you gain a deeper insight into precisely what you are feeling, its origin, and what to do to overcome them.

Curiosity About People

Whether you are an introvert or an extrovert, if you are emotionally intelligent, you will demonstrate curiosity about people around you. It is through this kind of curiosity that you can demonstrate empathy – a significant gateway to a high EQ. The more you show someone that you care about them and what they are experiencing, the more you will be curious about them.

You Embrace Change

If you are emotionally intelligent, then you have the flexibility and ability to constantly adapt to change. You will know that fear of change is the reason you will remain paralyzed and a major threat to your happiness and success in life. Look for the change that is going around you and then form a plan of action.

You Know Your Strengths and Weaknesses

When you are emotionally intelligent, you will not only understand emotions but also know what you are good at and what you are not yet skilled at. You will know who and what pushes your buttons within your surroundings so that you can position yourself better to achieve success. Having a high emotional intelligence means that you can lean on your strengths and leverage them to realize your potential, while raising your awareness of your weak points so that they don't hold you back from reaching your potential.

You Are a Good Judge of Character

Did you know that much of emotional intelligence boils down to social awareness? This is your ability to read people, know what they are all about, and gain a deeper insight into what they are going through. With time, this skill helps you become an exceptional judge of character, so that others don't remain a mystery to you. It allows you to know what makes them tick, understand the things that motivate them, and the things they try to hide beneath the surface.

You Are Hard to Offend

Having a strong grasp of who you are makes it hard for others to get under your skin. If you are emotionally intelligent, you are self-confident and have an open mind – two factors that help you develop a pretty thick skin. You can even poke fun at yourself or let other people make jokes about you, because you can draw a mental line between humor and degradation.

Letting Go of Mistakes

If you are emotionally intelligent, then you know better than to ruminate on your past mistakes. You can distance yourself from your mistakes without forgetting them. When you keep your mistakes at a safe distance, but are able to refer to them when the need arises, you position yourself to navigate future challenges and achieve success.

No one said that this was going to be a walk in the park. To walk this tightrope between remembering and ruminating, you must have a refined self-awareness. When you ruminate on your past mistakes you set yourself up for anxiety and becoming gun shy. On the other hand, forgetting all about your past mistakes makes it easy for you to repeat them again in the future.

The key to balancing these is to learn how to transform your failures into nuggets of improvement. This way, you create a tendency to bounce back up each time you fall.

Don't Hold Grudges

Did you know that when you hold a grudge, you activate negative emotions in response to stress? Well, every time you think of an unpleasant past event, the body goes into a fight-or-flight mode as a way to survive. This forces you to get up to either fight or run away when you are faced with a threat.

When the threat is imminent, this reaction is critical to your survival. However, when the threat is something that lies in the distant past, holding on to it will only wreak havoc on your body and in time negatively affect your health. According to research studies at Emory University, holding a grudge tends to raise our blood pressure and can cause heart disease.

In short, when you hold a grudge, you are holding on to stress. If you are emotionally intelligent, then you know tot stay away from this. When you let go of a grudge, it is not a sign of weakness. Instead, it makes you feel better and sets you up for improved health and overall wellbeing.

Neutralizes Toxic People

Dealing with difficult people is not only frustrating but also energy draining. With high emotional intelligence, you are in a better position to control your interactions with toxic people by ensuring that you can keep your emotions in check. When you must deal with a toxic person, you know the importance of approaching them rationally.

In other words, you can identify your emotions and ensure that your anger over frustrations does not get the best of you or fuel chaos. You also know that the other person has a point of view and that if you can hear where they are coming from, you will agree on a common ground and find a lasting solution. Even when things get completely derailed, people with high emotional intelligence can take toxic people with a grain of salt to ensure that they don't let themselves be brought down.

Don't Seek Perfection

Emotionally intelligent people don't set perfection as a goal because they know well that perfection does not exist. We are all human, and that fact alone makes us fallible. When you make perfection a goal, you are setting yourself up for a nagging feeling of failure that may make you give up or lower your efforts.

In other words, you end up spending much of your time complaining about your failures and what you could have done differently instead of moving on. Emotional intelligence allows you to view failure as a lesson to improve yourself without forgetting to celebrate every small achievement you have accomplished, so that you can stay motivated to achieve more in your future.

You Disconnect

When you can take regular breaks off the grid, this indicates high emotional intelligence. This is mainly because taking time off to reflect on yourself is one of the best ways to avoid stress and make sure you have things under control, so that you can live in the moment. Making yourself available 24/7 sets you up for constant barrage of stressors.

Force yourself to go offline from time to time to just breathe and do nothing. When you turn off your gadgets and just focus on yourself, you allow your mind and body to take a break. According to research, taking a break from technology, even simple tasks like reading emails, can reduce stress levels. Through technology, we can constantly communicate and are expected to be available 24 hours a day. This makes it difficult for you to enjoy a stress-free moment away from busy everyday life. When you take breaks, you allow yourself to have a change in your train of thought and relax without worrying about tasks that may appear on your phone.

Limit Caffeine Intake

When you are constantly drinking caffeine, you trigger the release of adrenaline, a source of the fight-or-flight response. It is this mechanism that makes it easy to avoid rational thinking in favor of something fast for survival.

This kind of survival mechanism is brilliant if a bear is chasing you. However, it is not needed when responding to emails. Taking too much caffeine throughout the day keeps your body in a constant hyper-aroused state of stress, so that your emotions begin to overrun your actions. With high emotional intelligence you know that caffeine is not good for you and avoid allowing it to get the best of you.

Get Enough Sleep

It is hard to overemphasize the importance of sleep in boosting your emotional intelligence and helping you manage your stress levels. Getting enough sleep every day plays a significant role in ensuring that you give the brain the time it needs to recharge, shuffle through the day's memories, store them, and discard anything that is not good for you. This ensures that once you get up, your brain is alert and ready to go!

People with high emotional intelligence understand that their self-control, memory and attention are reduced when they are sleep deprived. Therefore, ensure that from now on you make sleep your top priority.

Stop Negative Self-talk in Its Tracks

Are you allowing negative self-talk to hold you back from reaching your fullest potential? When you ruminate on negative thoughts, you are giving away your power to them. The trick is whenever negative thoughts come to your mind, ask yourself if they are facts or not.

When you feel like something "always" happens or "never" happens, realize that this is the brain's way of perceiving a threat. Emotionally intelligent people can separate their thoughts from facts to escape the cycle of negativity, gain a new perspective on life, and move on with optimism and positivity.

Won't Allow Anyone To Limit Your Joy

Do you let other people's opinions deprive you of your sense of pleasure and satisfaction? If you do, then realize that you are no longer the master of your happiness. Being emotionally intelligent means that whenever you feel good about something you have done, you will not let anyone's opinions or comments take away that good feeling.

Yes, it may be hard to switch off your reactions to what people say or think of you. However, you don't have to compare yourself to them. The trick is to take their opinions with a grain of salt. This way, no matter what others think, do or say about you, you allow your self-worth to rise from within you and take control of your thought process and actions.

Unlike IQ, you must note that emotional intelligence is malleable. As you train your mind to repeatedly practice new emotionally intelligent behaviors, you are promoting the growth of new pathways that turn them into habits. Your brain will start reinforcing the use of these behaviors and eliminate the connections to the old and destructive behaviors. Before you know it, you start responding to your environment with emotional intelligence automatically.

Importance of Emotional Intelligence

There are several benefits that emotional intelligence has to offer, most of which we will discuss in detail in the coming chapters. That said, emotional intelligence plays a key role in leading us on the path to a fulfilled and happy life. This is mainly by offering us a framework through which we can apply intelligence standards to our emotional responses and letting us understand these responses to ensure that they are logically consistent with our belief systems.

With constant changes in workplaces and in the available body of research, we must understand the art of emotional intelligence so that we can work with others in an organized way and as a team, respond effectively adapt to change and manage stress so that we can successfully achieve our business objectives. When you work on improving your emotional intelligence, you prepare yourself for personal happiness, professional success, and overall wellbeing.

Chapter 2:
The Four Attributes of Emotional Intelligence

Self-Management

You may be wondering what self-management has to do with emotional intelligence. One thing that is important to bear in mind is that self-management involves using what you know about your feelings so that you can manage them in such a way that they can generate positive interactions with the people around you. You want your emotions to motivate you in all situations. When you recognize that you have negative emotions you position yourself to be in control of your actions.

Think about it for a moment: if you are a manager at your workplace, do you think people would want to work with you if you don't have control over yourself and the way you react to situations? No one wants to interact with someone whose actions are informed by their prevailing mood. Achieving results by bullying and shouting at other people is is something that has no place in the modern world where people are aware of their rights and labor courts ensure that workers are properly treated.

I am not saying that self-management means that you can never be angry. We all go through situations that sometimes get on our nerves and it is perfectly reasonable to be angry. However, the key to being emotionally intelligent is to make sure that you are in control of your feelings and can channel them into solving problems.

Some people have a strong tendency to exaggerate the negative aspects of any given situation. If you are one of them, apply the reflective cycle in such situations so that you can have a realistic view of what is happening and what you can do to yield the desired result.

To engage your emotional intelligence, use your feelings in such a way that you can make constructive decisions about your actions. When you get stressed, it is easy to lose control of your emotions. It is easy to lose the ability to act appropriately and thoughtfully. To put this into perspective, take a minute to think back to a time when you were stressed and overwhelmed. Was it easy to think clearly? Did you make rational decisions at the time?

Probably not!

When you are stressed and overwhelmed, the ability to think clearly and to accurately assess your emotions tends to be compromised. Emotions are pieces of information that tell you about yourself and the people around you. However, in the face of stress and threat, they seem to take us out of our comfort zones and then we easily lose control of our abilities and ourselves.

Self-management ensures that you not only manage stress but also that you remain emotionally present in every situation so that your emotions don't override your thoughts and self-control. It allows you to make informed decisions that ensure you are on top of the situation, control impulsive emotions and actions, and manage them in a healthy way. Stress management allows you to take initiative, commit to the things that matter most in your life, follow through on these commitments, and adapt to changing circumstances.

Three Steps of Self-Management

Step 1 Identify What You Are Feeling

When you miss a meeting or delivery date, have problems with your spouse, or experience long-term sentiments that something is wrong, it is important that you identify the emotions you are feeling. Is it anger, sadness, anxiety, or frustration? Whatever your starting point is, learn how to exercise your self-awareness before you do something about it.

Step 2 Determine the Underlying Cause

This is often a very challenging step because you need to evaluate, reflect, and honestly find out the root cause of your feelings. Are you resentful of your boss because you have been told you missed the targets? Are you feeling sad, disappointed or frustrated because you suspect your spouse is having an affair? Find the root cause of your emotions.

Step 3 Act

Once you know what emotions you are feeling and where they are coming from, the next thing is for you to act. There is always something you can do to break out of the cycle of negative emotions. It can be something as simple as admitting the emotions you have are unjustified or misplaced, or that you are directing them at the wrong person.

When you recognize the truth behind your emotional feelings, you gain better control over them, so that you can manage them even when you are angry or stressed. Don't get me wrong – I am not saying that you should pretend as if these emotions are non-existent and dismiss them. No, accept that they are there and be willing to manage them.

When you master the art of self-management, you prepare yourself to think logically about every situation and decide on various ways you can handle them. This way you reduce the anger and fear you have and your level of emotional intelligence will rise above normal.

One thing you must bear in mind is that others will look to you for cues on what behavior is and is not acceptable. If you show you cannot control your own emotions, then you are telling them that there is no reason to control theirs. It is this lack of self-discipline that encourages people to copy undesirable habits – what Goleman refers to as "emotional hijacking." In other words, you let your mind be taken by your primitive emotions, and once they are standing in the way you cannot make a realistic and objective assessment of the situation.

These emotional breakdowns are building up gradually and unwillingly, and the symptoms are often overlooked. When you are frequently bullied and feel unsupported, your behavior may eventually result in negative consequences. However, when you make an honest evaluation of your actions and those of the people around you, you will not only identify what the problem is, but will also find possible solutions to the problem before it gets out of hand.

In other words, the key to develop your emotionally intelligent self-management is to conduct an honest evaluation of your behavior. Once you identify a negative form of behavior, you can work on removing or controlling it.

Think about it, do you often allow others' moods and attitudes to affect you? Are there times when you or any other member of your family or team has been influenced this way?

If so, make a conscious effort to isolate yourself so that you can be objective when evaluating a situation. Only a handful of people can have this kind of effect on you, and you likely know who they are. It could be because you have a personal relationship with that person that, in a way, is deeper than a usual working relationship. It could be someone you respect, closely identify with, or admire.

You realize that they influence your emotions. Knowing that plays a significant role in minimizing the negative influence their emotions might have on you, embracing who you are so that you can learn why their moods and attitudes affect you. When you have this knowledge, you can make a conscious effort to neutralize these negative emotions.

Tips to Improve Your Self-management Skills

- Breathe
- Differentiate between emotions and reason
- Share your goals with someone important in your life – a mentor or a spouse
- Count from one to ten
- Sleep on it
- Talk to someone you trust
- Laugh it out
- Think about it
- Talk better to yourself
- Visualize it
- Get enough sleep
- Control your body language
- Workout
- Control what you can and give up control over what you can't

What did Steve Jobs do when someone in the audience attacked him publicly during the Apple Developer Conference? He used some of the self-management tactics we have discussed here.

He paused for a couple of seconds before saying a word. He may or may not have counted to 10, but he paused and took a deep breath. This gave him time to compose himself, get a realistic perspective of the situation before he could say anything. He then took a sip of water and said: *"You know, you can please some of the people some of the time, but ..."*

Just doing that allowed his mind to change to a positive mindset. He then took another long pause – possibly to gather his thoughts on what to say next. You can do the same: be aware of your emotions and adequately manage your emotions. It is not about what other people say or think about you that matters; what counts is how you respond to their thoughts, actions, and words!

Self-Awareness

Emotional self-awareness is the second element of emotional intelligence. It refers to your ability to understand your emotions and how they affect your performance. Think about what is currently going on. How do you feel about it, why are you feeling that way? How is this helping or hurting what you are trying to achieve?

Self-awareness is also about how others see you and how you can align your image of yourself with the bigger picture. It is about having a clear sense of your strengths and weaknesses, something that gives you a realistic sense of self-confidence. It also gives you clarity on your values and purpose so that you can be more decisive when you set your course of action. As a leader, you can be candid, authentic, and speak with conviction about your vision.

Let us consider the following example where a chief tech officer at a company unwittingly bullies other workers. This officer is good at what she does, but struggles with managing others. She often plays favorites, tells people what to do, and does not seem to listen to what they have to say. Anyone she doesn't like is shut out. When confronted about this behavior, she denies it and denial and blames other people , saying they are the problem.

What do you think about this tech officer?

Well, she lacks emotional self-awareness.

According to research, a boss who is arrogant, stubborn, and a bully is often considered incompetent by their subordinates. These character traits have been shown to have a strong correlation with poor financial results, poor talent management and lack of motivation/inspiration to junior colleagues. They are poor team leaders.

A study by Korn Ferry Han Group reported that among leaders with various strengths in emotional self-awareness, at least 92% have teams with high energy and performance. In other words, when you are a great leader, you tend to create a positive emotional climate that stirs motivation and extra effort among employees – and this is because of a good emotional self-awareness. On the other hand, leaders with low self-awareness were reported to create a negative work climate on at least 78% of teams.

Bear in mind that emotional self-awareness is not something that you can achieve at one go and be done with it. It is instead a trait that you have to keep nurturing at every opportunity. It is an ongoing effort and a conscious choice that you make to be self-aware. The more you practice the more it gets ingrained and becomes natural. Being self-aware is simply regularly checking your sensory experience to allow a positive change in behavior.

The very first step to building your emotional intelligence is to raise awareness about your emotions. What you are currently feeling is often a mirror of what you experienced earlier in life. The ability to manage core emotions, such as anger, fear, joy, and sadness, all depends on the consistency and quality of your early life's emotional experiences. If your primary caretaker when you were a little child valued and understood your feelings, there is a high likelihood that your emotions are a great asset in your adult life. However, if it was the opposite, there is a chance that you will try to run away or hide from your emotions.

Take a minute to reflect on the following questions:

- Do you experience emotional feelings that flow and change from one moment to the next?
- Are your emotional feelings accompanied by strong physical sensations, such as chest pains, stomach cramps, or your throat constricting?
- Do you experience individual feelings and emotions, and do they show on your facial expressions?
- Can you experience intense feelings strong enough to capture your attention and that of others?
- Do you pay close attention to your emotional feelings, and do they inform your decision-making?

If none of these experiences ring a bell, then the chances are that you turned off or turned down your emotions. If you are going to build your emotional intelligence and become emotionally stable and healthy, it is important that you connect with your core feelings, embrace them, and get comfortable with them. The way to achieve this is by practicing mindfulness.

Being mindful is choosing to deliberately focus your attention on the present moment without judgment.

When you are mindful of what you are doing at that very moment, it shifts your attention and thoughts towards what you are doing at that moment so that you can appreciate the bigger picture. It can calm and focus your mind so that you are more self-aware.

Tips on How to Improve Your Self-awareness

Get Out of Your Comfort Zone

You might have heard the saying, "magic happens outside the comfort zone!" That is also true for emotions. If you look around, you will notice that there are instances where you run away from your feelings – and you are not alone. However, one thing to realize is that this is not a long-term plan. Allow your feelings to surface and offer the information they carry.

Instead of trying to shove your emotions away or running from them, learn how to guide yourself to them and through them. You cannot ignore what you are feeling because if you do, you are not doing yourself any good because they will only disappear now and resurface sometime later.

Be aware that getting out of your comfort zone is not all that bad. If you are going to expand your frontiers you have to develop the willingness to do things that might make you uncomfortable. Trust me, with practice you will start enjoying all the fruits of your labor.

Identify Your Triggers

Think of a trigger as anything – a substance, situation, person, or condition – that makes you emotional and prompts you to act in a certain way. You may, for instance, have a manager who feeds on others' energy like a vampire, and that makes you angry. It could be a noisy surrounding with your colleagues gossiping and laughing loudly over the phone when you need to concentrate on some work. It could be a colleague that lacks effective communication or people management skills.

Whatever it is, many people typically respond by shutting down. If this is something that happens to you in a place where emotional outbursts are considered a taboo, be aware that keeping those emotional feelings inside for yourself will do you no good. This is because your body language will be screaming, and someone may be sharp enough will notice.

When you learn to identify your triggers, you are preparing yourself for improved emotional intelligence. This is because you begin to learn how to improve your ability to control the outcome of your actions. You will learn how to calm down, take charge of your actions and keep your presence of spirit. To do that, identify the specific cases and begin generalizing from there. When you have a deeper understanding of what pushes your buttons, the situations become more manageable because the emotions you experience will not come as a surprise to you anymore.

It is also important that you go all the way at identifying the root cause of your triggers. In other words, you are finding out exactly why those people or situations get on your nerves. Why do you think a noisy surrounding triggers agitation or irritation? Is it because you are more skilled in reading and writing than you are in listening and talking? Or maybe the hate you have for your managers is because they remind you of a past manager who bullied you at the workplace? When you identify that your reactions are channeled to the wrong person, you might be able to get along with people better.

Don't Judge Your Feelings

Feelings are like waves of the ocean; they come and go. They are just what they are – feelings- nothing more, nothing less! Trying to label your feelings as either "good" or "bad," or as "positive" or "negative," will only decrease your ability to recognize them and raise your awareness of them. It is human nature to want to judge everything that comes your way and then put them in two boxes. Doing this will only make things counterproductive.

Everything you consider a "bad or negative" feeling will be something you want to avoid. There is some shame that comes with feeling bad or having negative feelings. On the other hand, when you have positive or good feelings, you want them to stay, and you may even see the need to reward yourself for having them. The problem is that you may let them run wild, which eventually drains you of your energy.

Whether the feeling is good or bad, or positive or negative, they bring certain information. Either you feel happy because you have achieved something, frustrated because the reality is different from what you expected, or sad because you lost something. However, if you allow your emotions to come and go just as they are – without judgment – then you might just have the chance to understand what they are and what the mind is trying to tell you. In other words, your emotions will just run their course and vanish without trying to control your actions.

Don't Make Decisions in a Bad Mood

There are times in life when we feel as though everything else is moving in the wrong direction. Whether you call this bad luck, feeling down, or depression, you cannot feel anything right because there is a black veil that clouds your thoughts.

The problem is that once the bad mood takes charge of your brain, it is easy to lose sight of the good things happening in our lives. You start to feel like you hate where you live, where you work, what you do, and the people around you irritate you. Even though you know deep down that what you think and feel is not true, you can't seem to get rid of these thoughts and emotions.

Emotional intelligence, through self-awareness, helps us to take note of the situation and accept it as it is. Admit that there is little to nothing you can do to change it. The trick is to wait – with time it will just pass. In other words, try to postpone making any life-changing decisions at this point, at least until you are out of this zone!

Don't Make Decisions in a Good Mood Either

This is the other side of the balance where you don't want to make major decisions just because you are feeling good – happy, ecstatic, or excited about something. Think about it: when you are walking down the streets and meet a salesman, they try to get you excited about what they are selling to the point that you lose control of your mind. This happens in such way that when they offer you their merchandise, they get you to feel so good about having it that you end up paying more for something that is not worth it.

I am not saying that feeling good is a bad thing. The point is, be careful of your good moods just as much as of your bad ones.

Get to the Birds-eye View

Have you ever heard someone tell you that you are "above things?" This is something applicable to emotional intelligence as well. Take a minute to imagine yourself rising above your personality so that you can watch yourself from above. Think of yourself soaring high like an eagle and then watching yourself from high up there – getting a bigger view of yourself from a viewer's eye. How many things do you think you will see and understand about yourself?

While you may not look at yourself from above, taking on an observer's view of yourself might just be what you need to understand your behavior. It will allow you to be aware of your thoughts and emotions in every situation you go through in life. Try to inject yourself with the trigger and reaction so that you can process the whole information and get a new perspective of things. The goal here is to constantly remind yourself of the real feelings under all the layers.

Revisit Your Values and Actions Accordingly

From my point of view, life is dynamic. The work we do every day is hard and our families are demanding. Even in the middle of all that, it is important that you set take time to learn something new, have fun, and be at peace. Get involved in activities that give you these things – such as playing sports with your kids, watching your favorite TV series, answering emails, and making phone calls to friends and family. All these activities fill your day. However, these things are also the reason why your focus is on the outside when you should look at what lies inside you.

One thing to keep in mind is that all these things on your to-do list can be overwhelming and draining all the energy you have left. The trick is to stop and review your values and actions.

Take time to ask yourself if your career is moving in the right direction or if your job requires you to do things you are not comfortable with, if your colleagues treat you right, whether you have enough time for the things that matter most in your life, or if your current path leads you where you would like to be in a couple of years.

All these things are not there to scare you about the present and the future, but instead to help you evaluate your values, trust, responsibilities, and determine if they are sustainable. The goal is how you wish to change the world and make it a better place for you and your family.

Check Yourself

It is important to understand that self-awareness is mostly an internal process and that there are external implications of what happens inside you. This is why you must learn to get in the habit of regularly checking yourself to make sure everything is okay.

Think about how your face looks like, if your eyes look puffy, if your makeup is right, if your clothes look well. Are you beginning to wrinkle? Is your working space tidy? Do you assume the right posture when working? Do you communicate with confidence? When walking, do you take long steps?

The trick is to make sure you are aware of your normal self and are alert for times when you feel stressed. Realize that everything changes, and when you are aware of the things happening in and around you, it becomes easy to identify stress factors fast enough before they can reach your conscious mind.

Fill Your Blind Spot With Feedback

Remember the windows of knowledge, which simply refers to the intimate parts of you that no one else knows about. Each one of us has three parts. What most of us are aware of are the private and the public parts of ourselves. However, what we fail to recognize is that blind spot, the part that we do not see.

Your view of yourself may not be impartial, but other people can see what you truly are. The question is, are you willing to seek help from others? Talk to someone you trust – spouse, partner, parent, or friend – to give you feedback about yourself. Be sure to observe this rule of communication: when you ask for feedback you should listen more than you talk. Open your heart to the truth, and instead of being defensive, let the people closest to you tell you truthfully their observations without trying to hold them back. One of the foundations of emotional intelligence is self-awareness. It is through self-awareness that you can learn how to spot your emotions, their root cause and your reaction to them. With time, you will learn how to control them so you can use them to serve your mind and its true purpose.

The last thing you want is to go through the motions of life without paying attention to your feelings. You don't want to ignore your feelings or allow them to control you and get the best of you. Realize that emotions are powerful forces that do either work miracles in your life or ruin your life completely. By mastering the art of self-awareness, you can finally take back the control of your life into your hands and steer it in the direction you want to go.

Social Awareness

It is one thing is to recognize and understand your emotional feelings, but another to accurately pick up and understand the emotions of others and what they are going through. If you are going to improve your emotional intelligence you must be willing to hold what you like so that you can practice social awareness. You have to stop talking, running monologues in your head, anticipating another person's answers before they can utter a word, and trying to create answers when someone is speaking.

Social awareness requires that you shift your focus from yourself to look out towards others, learn about them, and appreciate them. Social awareness is all about being grounded in our ability to recognize not only others' emotions but also understand them. While we may be tempted to focus only on our emotions, that will not work in environments that include other people. When you tune your emotions to other people, you allow yourself to pick up on vital signals to what is going on with them. This way you can read the room and measure your responses.

How can you do that?

Be Sure the Lens You Are Looking Through is Clear

This simply means that you must be there and ready to give others your undivided attention. Prepare yourself to take up the role of an observer by using your five senses and realizing that your sixth sense is your emotions.

Note that your emotions are important lenses for the brain and help you understand other people's signals. Be sure you are careful not to project your emotions onto others. Instead, use them as spider senses to stay alert and focus on what others are going through.

Watch Their Body Language

While someone may not always find the right words to express their feelings, body language is constantly communicating. According to research, it is not clear how much of the message is interpreted through body language. However, one thing to understand is that even if there is a disparity between words and body language, you believe the latter, right?

This is why when you are evaluating a person's body language you do a head-to-toe evaluation. Start with their eyes and let your eyes lock with theirs – are they blinking, shifting, or trying to look away? That might be indicative of deception, sadness, or depression. Look at their face, is their smile forced or authentic? What about their posture – is it upright or slumped? Are their hands fidgeting? All these cues help inform your social awareness when interacting with others.

Listen Carefully

Listening is one way of communicating. There is no way someone can talk nonstop without paying attention to what the other has to say – by listening. It is not just about words but also the tone of their voice, the speed at which these words are used, and the spacing between words.

When you are interacting with others, learn how to make a conscious effort to stop everything you are doing to just pay attention to what they have to say, how they say, and why they are saying it. When someone is speaking to you, stop answering an email, texting, or doing some other activity. Give them your undivided attention, observe, and listen so that you can accurately pick up every piece of information they are trying to deliver.

That said, social awareness goes a long way in helping us recognize and interpret non-verbal signals other people use when communicating a message. It is these cues that help you know what other people are feeling, how their emotions are changing every moment, and what is important to them.

Note that mindfulness is an ally of emotional and social awareness. To build your social awareness, recognize the important role of mindfulness in the social process. You will not be able to pick up nonverbal cues when you are trapped inside your head, thinking about things that don't matter. If you are going to be socially aware, then be present at the moment.

While you may pride yourself for your ability to multitask, it will cause you to miss subtle emotional shifts happening in other people, which eventually gets in the way of you understanding them. The trick is to leave your thoughts aside and focus on the interaction itself. Follow the flow of the other person's emotional response by realizing that it is a give-and-take process that calls for attention to changing emotional experiences.

By focusing on others, your self-awareness does not have to decrease. When you invest your time and efforts on others, you make it easier to gain a deeper insight into your emotional state, values, and beliefs. If you are uncomfortable hearing others express their views and opinions, you learn something important about yourself.

Relationship Management

This is about making your relationships effective, fulfilling, and fruitful. The trick to do that is by becoming aware of how effectively you can use nonverbal cues when communicating with others. It is almost impossible to avoid transmitting nonverbal messages to the people around us concerning your feelings and thoughts.

The muscles on your face – especially those around the eyes, forehead, mouth, and nose – play a significant role in conveying emotions without even using words. They also allow you to read other people's emotions. When you master how to use and interpret these signals, you can significantly improve your relationships.

The other way is by using humor and play to relieve stress. These are natural antidotes to stress, and they can lower the burden so that you can keep things in perspective. Laughter does not only relieve stress, but it also brings the nervous system into balance, calms the body, sharpens the mind, and makes you more empathetic.

Finally, learn to see conflicts as opportunities to get closer to others. In every human relationship conflict and disagreement are quite inevitable. You cannot possibly have your needs, expectations, and opinions met all the time – and that is not necessarily a bad thing. Conflict is good, and resolving them healthily and constructively goes a long way in strengthening trust between people. When conflict is not perceived as threatening, it can foster creativity, freedom, and safety of relationships.

Criteria for Effective Relationship Management

Decision

You make every decision regarding what the best course of action is in a given situation. This is something that should be informed by prior research you do to deepen your understanding of how others feel and why they feel that way.

You will have thoughts about varied ways of interacting with others and the different reactions you are likely to get when you say or do something. There is also a chance that you will be aware of the effect this has on you and how to properly manage it.

Interaction With Others

The way you interact with others should be based by your research and you could write it down or communicate with them face to face or through group discussions.

An Outcome

Realize that what you say or do and how you say it is informed by certain outcomes you desire to achieve. This is what makes relationship management an intentional activity.

Your Needs

Your desired results are guided by the particular needs you want to meet, one at a time.

Chapter 3:
Busting Myths About Emotional Intelligence

As a human being and a leader, it is difficult not to see the importance of emotional intelligence. It is because of emotional intelligence that I have achieved success both in business and life in general. It is this skill that has helped me see and understand my clients' pain points, create a positive working environment, and improve my relationships both in the workplace and outside.

However, despite emotional intelligence's popularity and usefulness, several myths surround it. It is a shame because it can be a powerful tool you can use to drive success and happiness into your life. Here are some of the misconceptions about emotional intelligence that you can let go of so that you can make the most of your career and life.

Emotional Intelligence Does not Exist

There are people – including psychologists – who believe that there is no such thing as emotional intelligence. Emotional intelligence is a relatively new concept, and different people have different ways of defining what it is. One thing to bear in mind is that testing for emotional intelligence is not a scientific thing to do.

Emotional intelligence is real, and it is something that dates back to the '30s and '40s when people were trying to express their interest in this area. Edward Thorndike came up with the term social intelligence and explained how this was an essential component in our lives and in ensuring that we succeed in what we do. Several other people contributed to emotional intelligence until Goleman took it to the next level in 1995.

Even though it took a journalist to spread the concept across to the masses, psychologists have been trying to understand this concept for decades. While some believe that this is not something that exists, there are several other experts who strongly believe and demonstrate its existence.

It is All About Empathy

Even after decades of writing and speaking to people about the science of emotional intelligence, it is interesting that there still are people who believe in one or more emotional intelligence myths. What is shocking is that most people think that emotional intelligence is all about empathy.

While empathy is a component of emotional intelligence, it is only a slice of the whole ability. It is much more complicated than just being charmingly empathic. It is the capacity to recognize your feelings and those of the people around them, how to manage these emotions, and how to effectively interact with others. It is through emotional intelligence that one learns how to strike a healthy balance between social, emotional, and intelligence competencies.

It is Not About Awareness But Behavioral Change

According to researchers, raw knowledge in itself is not about a change in behavior. For instance, we all know that smoking, eating fast foods every day and lack of physical exercise are bad for our health. Even with this knowledge people still need to be motivated to change their habits so that they can make choices that support their overall wellbeing. It is about calling people into the right kind of environment for the desired result to take place.

Just because you are aware of someone else's feelings does not mean that you have high emotional intelligence. It is about using this knowledge you have and the motivation to do it and the right environment that supports your actions.

If you are a manager, you can use emotional intelligence to your advantage during the hiring process. While it would not hurt to screen people's levels of emotional intelligence, what is ideal is to train them and equip them with the right skills to improve their EQ. From now on, you can build culture and surroundings where these skills are put to use.

Emotional Intelligence is Equated with Other Personality Traits

There is no way you can equate emotional intelligence to such personality traits as optimism, calmness, kindness, motivation and happiness, among others. Even though these personality traits are very important and help us achieve success in our lives, they have very little to do with intelligence. They have very little to do with emotions and absolutely nothing to do with actual emotional intelligence.

Unfortunately, there are trained psychologists who tend to confuse emotional intelligence with character traits. These personality traits should be called exactly what they are instead of mixing them up in an assortment named emotional intelligence.

Emotional Intelligence Predicts Success

For decades, people have thought that those who are most successful in life are emotionally intelligent. While it is easy to see how emotional intelligence influences how a person communicates, leads, and negotiates, research shows that we tend to do business with people we choose and like.

Yes, emotional intelligence plays a significant role in one's success, but it is not the only indicator/predictor. Take a look at all the top successful people across the world and rate them one by one – you'll be surprised to find that most of them don't lack even an ounce of emotional intelligence.

People are diverse, and there are equally diverse ways one can achieve success, become accomplished leaders, enjoy a successful professional life, and build a brilliant company. Unfortunately for some, emotional intelligence is not part of the equation. According to research published in the Journal of Applied Psychology there is no correlation between emotional intelligence and job performance.

You Either Have EI, or You Don't

Some people believe that emotional intelligence is innate. In other words they strongly think that it is something you are born with or without. However, emotional intelligence is something that anyone can learn and develop.

Yes, it may not happen overnight, but you can become emotionally intelligent if you continually practice self-awareness, relationship management, social awareness, and self-management. It is through these skills that you can master how to channel your emotions in the right direction and for the right reasons. The best way to start is to become mindful of your words and know your triggers. Once you step up your empathy skills, you will be on your way to achieving emotional intelligence.

You Have to Give Up Emotional Intelligence to Be Mentally Tough

Over the last couple of years, several people have discussed the importance of mental toughness. This is commonly directed towards people who have served in the army, specifically the Navy Seals and Marines.

I have found this advice to be useful to help yourself strengthen your focus and resilience. However, when it comes to emotional intelligence, mentally tough people tend to ignore their emotions and those of the people around them. This conflicts with the misconceptions that emotions are a sign of weakness.

If you cannot raise your awareness of your feelings and those of people around you, you cannot say that you are emotionally intelligent. Rather than trying to be mentally tough, you must not allow other people to use your emotions against you. For instance, if you see a high-performing athlete, they might seem that they are in the "zone," but they have no idea what is happening around them. They tend to keep a cool head just until the game is over.

Realize that mental toughness is not just about driving stricter timelines. It is about taking a pause to just listen to what lies inside you, so that you have a better understanding of yourself and those around you and where they are coming from. It is about having the discipline not to get too immersed in emotions.

There is no Dark Side to Emotional Intelligence

Whenever we talk about emotional intelligence, it is always about something positive. However, just like with any other force, there is always a light and dark side. A good example of this is leaders who drum-up fear just to satisfy their own selfish needs. In this case, it would be to keep employees in check or just have people vote for them.

When people hone their emotional skills, they increase their likelihood of manipulating others. This is mainly because when you can control your emotional feelings you tend to mask your true feelings. When you know that other people are experiencing certain feelings, chances are you will pull on their heartstrings and motivate them to go against their best interests.

This does not mean that you should start being wary of emotional intelligence. If you have boosted your emotional intelligence, you will be in a better position to identify when someone else is trying to cover your eyes and cloud your judgment.

It Does not Influence Our Decisions

In reality, it is not possible to decide without having an emotional bias. Every feeling starts with an external stimulus regardless of what someone has said or what the physical events are. From that point on, the brain generates a feeling that causes the body to produce responsive hormones. These hormones, in turn, enter the bloodstream to create a positive or a negative feeling.

There is no Correlation Between Emotional Intelligence and Physical Wellbeing

According to research studies, having a higher emotional intelligence is associated with improving the psychological and physical health of an individual. This is something that you and I could take for granted, right?

Having the ability to notice, understand, and fix our moods goes a long way to ensure that we make healthier decisions in life. For instance, if you are stressed you might feel the need to turn to comfort foods, cigarettes, alcohol, or something else, just to try and overcome that emotion. Unfortunately, all these things you are turning to are unhealthy vices. The worst part is that when you ignore these emotional feelings, you start experiencing symptoms such as fatigue, stomach pain, muscle tension, and other potentially life-threatening conditions like heart disease.

Chapter 4:
Steps on How to Grow Emotional Intelligence

Step 1 Tapping Into Your Emotions

Note Your Emotional Reactions to Events Throughout the Day

It is easy to place your emotional feelings on your experiences throughout the day. One thing you should note is that taking the time to acknowledge how you feel about your experiences is critical to improving your emotional intelligence. Ignoring your feelings means that you are ignoring important information that has a significant impact on your mindset and how you carry yourself. Choose to focus your attention on your emotional feelings so that you can easily connect them to your experiences.

For instance, imagine you are at the workplace in a meeting and suddenly a colleague interrupts you when you are still presenting your point. What emotions are you likely to experience? If you are being praised for the good work you have done, what would you feel?

When you get into the habit of naming your emotions as they happen, you raise your awareness of the surroundings and each experience you go through along with the emotions those experiences stir up. This way, you start to gradually increase your emotional intelligence.

The trick is for you to get in the habit of tapping into your emotions throughout the day. Think about how you feel when you wake up and before you go to bed, and make it a habit.

Pay Attention to your Body

Rather than trying to ignore the physical manifestations of your emotional feelings, start listening to them. Realize that your mind and body are interconnected, and neither can survive without the other. In other words, the body and the mind deeply influence each other.

To raise your emotional intelligence, learn how to read physical signals and use them to find out what emotions you are experiencing. For instance, when you are stressed, you might feel like there is a knot in your stomach, a tightening on your chest, or paced breathing. When you are sad, it might feel like getting up with slow and heavy limbs. When you are happy or anxious, you might feel butterflies in your stomach or your heart racing fast.

Observe How Your Emotions and Behavior are Connected

Take a minute to reflect on the last time you felt a strong emotion; how did you react?

Often, when we feel strong emotional feelings, we try to mask them so that we don't have to deal with them, much less have people realize that we are going through something. Emotional intelligence is about tuning into your gut feeling in every situation you experience every other day, instead of choosing to react without taking the time to reflect.

Note that the deeper your understanding of what triggers your impulses, the more you increase your emotional intelligence to be in a better position to use what you know to change your future behavior.

Here are a couple of examples of behaviors and what underlies them:

- Feeling embarrassed or insecure has a likelihood of making you withdraw from others and from engaging in conversations.
- When you are angry you might realize your voice rises or angrily turns away.
- When you are overwhelmed, you might panic and lose track of what matters most in your life.

Avoid Judging Your Own Emotions

Do you know that every emotional feeling you have is valid – even if it is negative? One thing to note is that even if your emotions are negative, judging them will only inhibit your ability to fully feel them and hence to use them positively.

Think of it this way – every emotion you are feeling carries bits and pieces of information connected to something that is happening around you. Without this information, you will remain in the dark about what is the right way to react. This explains the reason our ability to feel our emotions is a form of intelligence.

Yes, this is not something you will master overnight, but with the practice of letting go of negative emotions, you can effectively connect them to what is happening around you. For instance, if you are bitterly envious, the first thing you need to ask yourself is what that emotion is telling you about the whole situation. It is also important that you fully experience every positive emotion. Try to connect your satisfaction or happiness to what is happening in your life so that you can master how to feel them.

Notice Patterns in Your Emotional History

It is one thing to learn about recognizing your feelings, but it is quite the other to connect them to your experiences. When you have a strong emotion, it is important to try and reflect on the time you last felt that way. Try to assess what happened before, during, and after the event.

This will help you see a pattern so that you can exert more control over your behavior. Take note of how you handled the situation before and what the outcome was. This way you can make a better decision this time to handle the situation differently, so that you can get the desired result. It is also important to keep a journal of emotional reactions and how you feel with each passing day so that you can determine if there is a pattern in the way you react to situations.

Practice Deciding How to Behave

One thing to keep in mind is that you cannot help the emotions you feel. However, you can choose to stay connected to everything that is happening around you. Without this set of information, you are likely to be left out in the dark about how you can appropriately react. This is why having the ability to feel your emotions is a form of intelligence.

When something unpleasant happens in your life, take a moment to feel your emotions. Allow that wave of sadness and anger to wash over you. Once that wave is gone, the next thing is for you to decide on the appropriate course of action. Instead of repressing your feelings, communicate them or keep trying, instead of throwing in the towel.

Don't try to escape your emotions. Yes, letting your negative feelings rise to the surface may not be the best thing to do, and you may be tempted to control them by drinking, burying your head in movies, or turning to habits that numb your pain. When you do this, your EQ will start going down.

Step 2 Connecting with Other People

Be Open-minded and Agreeable

When it comes to emotional intelligence, being open and agreeable go hand in hand. When you have a narrow mind, you are generally saying that you have a low EQ. However, when you allow your mind to be open you not only gain understanding and reflect on what is happening internally, but it also gets easier to handle conflicts in a self-assured and calm manner. You will become socially aware of what others are going through, and possibilities will begin to open to you.

One of the best ways you can strengthen your EQ is to listen to debates on radio or television. Ensure that you consider both sides of the argument and find out what subtleties require your close inspection. When someone fails to react the same way you would, don't be mad at them. Instead, consider the reasons they reacted that way and try to see things from their perspective.

Improve Your Empathy Skills

Empathy simply refers to the ability to recognize how others are feeling so that you can share emotions with them. When you are an active listener, you can pay attention to what others are saying so that you get a better sense of what they are feeling. In other words, you are using the situation to make informed choices that will help improve your relationships – and that is a sign of emotional intelligence.

If you want to grow your empathy, be willing to put yourself in the other person's shoes. Try to think about how you would react if you were in the same situation. When you actively imagine what it must be like to experience the same situation, you will not only identify with their hardship but will also see ways to help them through support and care.

Whenever you see someone experiencing strong emotions, the first thing you need to ask yourself is how you would react in the same situation. Being truly interested in what the other person is saying or experiencing helps a great deal in ensuring that you react more sensitively. Rather than allowing your thoughts to drift from side to side, ask yourself questions and put what they are saying in summary form so that they know that you are in the conversation with them.

Read People's Body Language

Read between lines and pick up what the other person is truly feeling by focusing on their body language and facial expressions. There are times when people say things when their body language and facial expression are saying a different thing. Practice being observant so that you can pick up on what is less obvious – because that is where people's emotions lie.

If you are not sure that you can accurately interpret another's body language and facial expressions, try taking a quiz. When they raise their voice, it indicates that they are not only stressed but also angry about the whole situation.

See the Effect You Have on Others

When it comes to emotional intelligence, understanding other people's emotions is only half the battle. It is important that you also understand what effect you have on them. When you are around people, do you tend to make them nervous, anxious, angry, or cheerful? When you walk into a room where people are having a discussion, do they get enthusiastic and open up more, or do they retract and end the conversation?

When you put these things into perspective, you will not only identify the patterns you need to change but also see how you can appropriately change to improve the situation. If you are someone who tends to pick fights with loved ones or cause people to close up when you are around them, consider changing your attitude so that you can improve the emotional effect you have on others.

Start by asking your loved ones what they think about your emotionality and where you can improve, so that you become a better person. It could be your tone of voice, listening skills, or something else. Whatever it is, you can ask people you trust to help you recognize the effect you have on others and how they can help you change for the better.

Practice Being Emotionally Honest

When someone tells you that they are "fine" with a frown, it means they are not communicating honestly. Sometimes you are the person on the other side of a conversation. One thing to realize is that for people to read you better, you have to be able to physically open up about your emotions. When you get into an argument, tell people that you are angry, upset, or disappointed in them. When something is making you happy, share that happiness and joy with the people around you.

When you are yourself, you make it easier for other people to get to know you better. People will tend to trust you more when you show them where you are coming from. That said, one thing to remember is that there is a line: learn to control your emotions so that you don't hurt the people around you.

Step 3 Putting EQ to Practical Use

See Where You Have Room for Improvement

In life, being intellectually capable is very important. However, being emotionally intelligent is an essential need. When you have high emotional intelligence, you are in a better position to seize job opportunities as they present themselves or lead a better relationship. The four core elements of emotional intelligence we have discussed in the previous chapter will help you figure out where you need improvement in your life. Is it self-awareness, self-management, social awareness, or relationship management? Whatever it is, you can work on improving it and boost your emotional intelligence.

Lower Your Stress Level by Raising Your EQ

When you hear someone say that they are stressed, what they are saying is that they are feeling overwhelmed by a wide range of emotions. Life is filled with difficult situations ranging from relationship breakups to job loss. In between these things are millions of stress triggers that have the potential of making any daily issue a challenge. If you are stressed a lot, it is hard to behave the way you want to. However, when you have a plan in place to help you relieve stress, you stand a chance of improving your emotional intelligence and all aspects surrounding it.

What triggers your stress? What can you do to help alleviate your stress? Create a list of all forms of stress relief from hanging out with friends to taking a walk to enjoy nature. That said, if you feel that your stress levels are getting out of hand, consider getting the help you need from a professional therapist. They can give you the tools you need to cope with stress and raise your EQ in the process.

Be More Light-hearted at Home and Work

When you have optimism, it becomes easier to see the beauty in life. It becomes easy to turn your awareness into everyday objects so that you can share your emotional feelings with the people in your life. Trust me, no one wants to sit down and spend time with someone who has no optimism.

When you are optimistic, you draw people to yourself and enjoy all the possibilities these connections have to offer. On the other hand, if you are negative you will push people away instead of building your resilience. Emotionally intelligent people know how to use their humor and fun to make themselves and the people around them feel happier and safer – and they can use laughter to get through tough situations.

Chapter 5:
Emotional Intelligence at School/Workplace

Each passing day, we all make emotionally charged decisions. Each time we are planning something we feel as though our plan A is better than plan B and end up making choices based on our gut instincts or emotions. However, when we understand where these emotions are coming from in the first place, only then will we become in harmony with each other – especially when working in a team.

With the increase in globalization, emotional intelligence has found a significant place in our lives because places at school or work have become more cross-cultural and global. It is because of globalization that our interactions have become complex along with how we express these emotions.

One thing to remember is that emotional intelligence in school or at the workplace comes down to expressing, understanding and managing good relationships and addressing problems even when you are under intense pressure from above.

Today, the conventional measure of intelligence pays attention to logic and reasoning in such areas as math and reading comprehension. The general idea that this kind of reasoning is what determines our success and productivity at the workplace is persuasive and intuitive as well. This is mainly because it measures our ability to grasp and digest facts in our surroundings.

However, the idea that there is only one form of intelligence has recently been subjected to intense scrutiny. Many psychologists now have the theory of multiple intelligences. The two major areas that are measured in tests include verbal-linguistic intelligence and logical-math intelligence. But these are only two areas out of nine different areas of intelligence with varied characteristics.

That said, not all these intelligences have found their way into the world of business. For instance, bodily-kinesthetic intelligence is what most dancers, athletes, and other forms of physical labor use. It is through this form of intelligence that minds have been opened to greater possibilities of thinking and achieving success.

On the other hand, the ideas about rational intelligence took root from the enlightenment that happened soon after scientific thoughts were codified for the very first time. The very early aspect used by natural philosophers was the idea of rational objectivity, which required that individuals attempt to view the world around them not as they desire it to be but as it is. While this idea may seem perfect on the surface, the problem is that it often causes people to move away from using their gut feelings and using their emotions in finding solutions to real-life problems. It is important to note that rational intelligence does not only focus on hard facts, but also logical reasoning that results from unproductive scenarios of win-lose cases.

In today's workplace, excelling means striking a balance between interpersonal and intrapersonal intelligence. The former simply refers to the ability to detect and respond to other people's emotions, moods, desires, and motivations. On the other hand, the latter simply refers to the ability to raise our awareness of self so that we are more aligned with our beliefs, values, and thought processes.

When you combine these concepts, you get a good overview of emotional intelligence and how it is related to business leadership. When you don't have the guiding influence of rational intelligence, emotional intelligence ends up being subjective in such a way that it is no longer useful for business goals. However, if properly treated, it serves as a key to drive internal collaborations and external alliances.

EI is the Key to Communication in the Workplace and School

In its most refined form, emotional intelligence offers empathy, which is important to help us to fully understand others' perspective even when it contradicts our own view of things. According to research, there is evidence that shows women who have high emotional intelligence tend to act in collaborative ways by embracing an inclusive leadership style, as compared to men.

It does not matter whether you are a man or a woman when you practice emotional intelligence. There are so many more benefits it has to offer at the workplace and to all stakeholders across the industry. This is by:

- Helping leaders to motivate and inspire good works among its employees by understanding other people's motivators.
- Bringing more people to the table and helping one avoid the traps of group thinking.
- Empowering leaders to not only recognize possibilities, but act on opportunities that other people may not be aware of in the first place.

- Assisting in conflict identification and resolution in such a fair and even-handed manner.
- Producing higher morale and helping other people to make the most of their professional potential.

Just like rational intelligence, emotional intelligence is something you and I can cultivate if we put in effort and take the time to study it. The very first step to developing emotional intelligence is by strengthening your power of introspection. It is about recognizing your emotional feelings, thought processes, and biases, so that whenever you are making decisions they are not only informed but well-rounded. When you exercise emotional intelligence, act in confidence, rise above your fears and worries, and be able to question the status quo and avoid gut reactions.

Emotional Intelligence in Hiring Processes

Even though technical skills are things that can be imparted through training, it is more challenging to teach emotional intelligence during the recruitment process at the workplace. While companies can integrate theories of emotional intelligence in their hiring processes and professional development in all spheres, it is not easy to achieve that with a 100% accuracy.

For instance, when hiring entry-level employees, you may wish to test for their EQ when you have a group of candidates competing for the same new position or a promotion. Most managers, leaders, and stakeholders identified as having high emotional intelligence and high leadership potential tend to deliver better results as part of their development process.

Even though most roles at the workplace could benefit from emotional intelligence, not all roles require highly developed emotional intelligence. The higher one climbs in the career ladder; the more valuable emotional intelligence becomes.

This explains why professionals such as the Human Resource or Public Relations departments benefit a lot from emotional intelligence, because they are mostly involved in the hiring process. This is mainly because their emotional development plays a significant role in helping companies maximize their contributions and optimize their investments for future growth and development.

Emotional Intelligence in the Globalized Economy

Just as the global economy has developed into a system of partnerships, negotiations and communications, emotional intelligence plays a bigger role in the public sphere. This is why emotional intelligence is strongly correlated to such traits as self-control, perseverance, and increased performance and productivity, even under pressure. Leaders with emotional intelligence have the emotional strength to adjust and adapt to change, deal with setbacks, and achieve goals.

It does not matter how the economy changes. What matters most is that conventional intelligence will always be the center of success in the global economy. That said, bear in mind that even the most technical of all roles requires one to greatly expand networks with diversified stakeholder portfolios, taking up roles in complex atmospheres and investing both emotional and mental capital to handle the most unexpected of situations. Both rational and emotional intelligence are here to stay, and it takes brilliant leaders, managers, and students to exhibit both.

Chapter 6:
Emotional Intelligence and Health

Physical Health

According to research, there is evidence that shows emotional intelligence has a significant and direct impact on our physical health. Instead of using a traditional aspect of emotional intelligence, use a trait meta-mood scale (TMMS) that directly relates to the core aspect of EQ;

Attention

This refers to the ability to take note and focus our attention on our feelings.

Clarity

This simply refers to the ability to clearly understand the nature of your moods.

Repair

This refers to the ability to maintain a positive mood and repair negative emotions as necessary to achieve your goals.

When you look at things from this perspective, what you will note is that emotional intelligence can affect physical health. For instance, you have the power of attention, clarity, and repair. There is a high likelihood that the following scenario holds to you.

First, you could begin to feel easily irritable and cannot seem to put your mind on one thing. After a couple of considerations, you realize that you didn't have your breakfast because you woke up late and had to prepare the kids for school and get ready for work. You realize that all you have had are two cups of coffee since you woke up. What you are essentially feeling is hunger pangs. You decide to take a break to go into the breakroom to fix yourself a healthy snack because you can't wait until lunch, which is still two hours away.

In the above example, you paid attention to your mood, identified the reason that underlies it, and exerted your effort into repairing the negative emotions you were feeling before they got out of hand – by coming up with a solution that would address your needs and contribute to your desired outcome.

What do you notice about this example? Emotional intelligence positively affects one's health.

Several research studies that have been conducted relate the elements of emotional stress and the behavioral response of cardiac, hormonal and enzymatic activity. Some research participants are writing about their traumatic emotional events – including recall and evaluation. During these sessions, their blood pressure was measured.

Without offering an exhaustive account of the research studies, the results showed that people who accurately perceive their emotional feelings could cope with stressful situations. They also demonstrated the ability to overcome hesitancy by seeking medical help, accepting changes in their bodies, and proactively seeking a resolution to achieve better health.

This is something that can be done with such habits as an improved diet, overcoming alcohol addiction, and a regular workout regimen. All these behavioral patterns are associated with strong emotional intelligence, increased level of dynamism, acceptance of personal reality, and responsibility for your own well-being.

In other words, self-awareness, motivation, and self-management increase your likelihood of enjoying a positive health regardless of how and when they manifest in your life.

Mental Health

According to research, mental health conditions are linked to lower levels of emotional intelligence. For instance, someone with borderline personality disorder (BPD) has shown greater sensitivity to expressing emotional feelings. What is interesting is that people with BPD often struggle to label their emotions and what they truly mean. The outcome of this is that they cannot seem to control their emotions.

People with depression have been shown to have lower EQ score on average. These people tend to show less sensitivity to changing emotional contexts, hence causing them to get stuck in negativity.

Social anxiety has also been linked to a low EQ. People with social anxiety tend to fear what others will think or say about them. They have a high likelihood of perceiving neutral expressions like hostility, which causes them to misinterpret social signals.

The other thing that is important to note is that substance abuse contributes to serious deficits in aspects related to emotional intelligence. Unlike the conditions we have already mentioned, drug abuse contributes to impaired emotional perception and regulation.

Interestingly, research studies have shown that there is a link between low emotional intelligence and self-destructive habits. In other words, some people use self-harm as a way of attempting to regulate their emotions.

By improving your emotional intelligence, you significantly impact your mental health, so that people can have reduced tendencies for aggression and quickly recover from trauma.

This explains why mental health awareness is on the rise and risks reaching proportions that will exceed available services. While there have been more studies on mental health, no one should doubt the fact that we need more information and resources in this area. Mental health challenges can occur for anyone of any age, gender, profession, or culture. There are several reasons mental health issues occur, and yet all cases are different.

That is why we propose emotional intelligence in support strategies that help people recover from mental health issues. Don't get me wrong; I am not saying that you should replace therapy and medical attention with emotional intelligence. However, people with mental issues at the lower end of the spectrum could greatly benefit from EI.

Through self-awareness, you can identify your strengths and weaknesses and leverage them to your advantage. When you know your weak areas, you can better position yourself to improve your mental balance. Remember that self-awareness is a central component of emotional intelligence and has been tested in a wide range of fields. When someone has mental health problems, increasing their awareness of their emotions allows them to recognize their issues before they can get out of hand – prevention is better than cure!

That is why self-awareness is integral to our mental balance. For instance, if you are aware of your emotions and actions and can recognize that there are certain areas where you need help controlling your emotions, you can learn how to effectively manage them. This is because your awareness will focus on your emotional feelings and the strategies you can use to manage them. Instead of taking on more tasks than you can handle, you take on projects you can complete, lower stress levels, and achieve mental balance. Doing this will not only help you get better but will also improve your self-confidence, create positivity, enhance your mindset, facilitate balance and happiness in your life.

There are so many ways you can improve your mental state and boost your emotional intelligence. One of them is through the practice of mindfulness. Mindfulness plays a significant role in helping people deal with their current situations. For instance, when you pause to just take in a deep breath, you not only allow your mind to shift to the present moment, but also allow your mind and body to regain balance and more control.

The other way you can achieve mental balance is through meditation. While not everyone will feel comfortable with meditation, it is very effective. You do not have to be religious to practice meditation. When you meditate you give focus and scope to your mind. It needs to deal with emotional imbalance. Mental health challenges are associated with a lack of energy and motivation. However, when you meditate and allow your mind to feed on positive self-talk and affirmations, you not only release all negativity but also allow the mind to see possibilities where the balance was lacking.

Yes, someone with mental health issues might not feel positively changing their thought process. However, small changes here and there go a long way in bringing positivity into your life. Instead of thinking that you cannot do something, you can simply turn that into something positive like *"I've got what it takes to do this."*

The other trick is to use music, something that has been shown to boost emotional intelligence. It does not only improve one's mood and emotions but also encourages one to use a reflective process, which offers you the opportunity to evaluate yourself, your emotions, thoughts, and progress.

For you to grow you must learn to motivate yourself to meet both your intrinsic and extrinsic needs – which can be physical, mental, nutritional, physiological or a combination of all. The best way to use motivation is to effectively direct it through the use of process goals. Within the facet of mental health, one of the key drivers is the use of motivation to create energy. According to research, when you have no motivation you risk developing mental health challenges. Adopt motivation strategies such as positive self-talk and goal setting to reverse this trend.

Finally, how many friends do you have? Are these quality friendships? It is one thing to have many friends but it is quite another to have friends who look out for you and who help you become a better person. This is what quality friendship is all about and is the kind of support needed by those experiencing mental health challenges. To improve your emotional intelligence, look for opportunities to meet new people and build new relationships. While this is something that can be challenging for people with mental health issues, positioning yourself within the right time and space makes it possible, when your purpose of building new friendships and growing the existing ones allows you to open up and achieve consistency of trust.

Chapter 7:
Emotional Intelligence and Relationships

The secret to lasting relationships is emotional intelligence. This is mainly because emotional intelligence makes people extremely aware of changes happening around them, small or big. When you build your emotional intelligence, you boost your sensitivity that we all are seeking in our partners. Through active awareness and empathy, you will gain the ability to sense when there is a slight change in the dynamics of your romance so that you can act accordingly.

Realize that you have the potential to attain the kind of love you have always dreamed of. You have the potential to participate in a relationship in which you enjoy deep intimacy, real commitment, mutual kindness, and soulful caring. This is because of empathy – our innate ability to share our emotional experiences with others.

For anyone to reach this height of intimacy and romance, you need all the skills of high emotional intelligence: sharp emotional awareness, acceptance, and a vigilant active social awareness. Your emotional awareness will help you avoid making mistakes as a result of getting lustful or intoxicated in love. Acceptance, on the other hand, goes a long way in helping us experience emotions that have the potential of harming us if left unattended. Finally, active vigilance is what helps us to evaluate our relationship so that we know what is working and what is not.

So, how can we build emotionally intelligent romantic relationships?

One thing to realize is that you don't have to choose the wrong lovers and end up in a failed marriage. You don't have to sit back and watch romance decline in your long-term relationship. Look inside your relationship and determine whether there are conflicting needs and wants that might come between you and your partner. You deserve a loving and healthy relationship filled with romance. The last thing you want is to resign yourself to boredom or fighting in your love life.

You have the potential to attain the kind of love you have always wanted. This does not mean that your emotional intelligence should be at a peak before you can find love. Research shows that falling in love helps most people stay motivated to educate their hearts. This explains why most deeply passionate lovers are in their eighties because they find out that a high emotional intelligence in both partners adds up to romance that never stops growing, does not lose its spark, and always seeks to strengthen them, both individually and collectively.

Here are some ways you can boost the EQ in your relationship.

Actively Seek Change in Your Relationship

Look around you. Most people you know may be in relationships, but most do not like change. People fear change because they think that it will destroy their romance and attraction to each other. However, the opposite is true. Change helps you realize everything you have been missing.

One thing to keep in mind is that change does not necessarily have to mean worse. Research shows that things often come out better than ever on the other side of change. Think of your romantic relationship as an organism that by nature, must change. It is through change that a relationship gets to grow. Your ability to embrace change plays a significant role in helping you gain courage and a sense of optimism.

Take a minute to think about your relationship. What is it that your partner needs most from you? Is it something new? Do you need time to reassess things together? Are there external influences in your life that are demanding some change in the roles in your relationship? Do you consider yourself happier than you used to be?

Without emotional intelligence, these questions are challenging and scary to answer, and that is the reason why lovers often ignore the signals of necessary change until the problems are out of control.

Look at Challenges as Opportunities Instead of Problems

Did you know that courage and optimism are what help people view dilemmas as challenging opportunities rather than problems?

Take a minute to think about how creative you and your partner can be. This is the point where you don't need to blame each other for emotions. In other words, you are not controlled by negative emotional influences. You are simply alert enough not to repeat the mistakes you have made in the past.

With high emotional intelligence you are free from resignations and routine, so that you start looking at problems as opportunities for growth. You are not afraid when the problem comes up because you know that you can simply come down and do some brainstorming to solve the problems. You view differences as opportunities to come together and get closer, so that you can both come out on the other side of victory stronger, together and individually.

Respect All the Feelings You Have for Each Other

None of us is delighted by all the discoveries we make about our partners over time. However, one thing to realize is that when it comes to emotions, you must accept them all. Falling in love with someone does not mean that you will never be angry, disappointed, jealous, or hurt.

It is up to you how you respond to these emotions. What matters the most is that you feel them. Several relationships have been ruined by blame, and millions of couples have dismissed their need for deep intimacy because of shame. These are cruel reminders of fear, anxiety, and anger. If you have done what it takes to build your emotional intelligence, you will choose to experience the emotions together so that you can get on with your lives together.

Keep Laughter in Your Love Life

Several couples intellectualize their emotions without even realizing it. If you are one of them, realize that acceptance is what you need, and a large part of that comes with lots of laughter. To be accepted in your relationship, learn to laugh with each other.

If you cannot laugh together, chances are you will not be able to stand each other's unique flaws and inevitable stumbling blocks any more than you can tolerate your own. You will not have the ability to accept surprises no matter how pleasant they might be. However, when you work on growing your emotional intelligence you will not only ensure that you constantly improve your relationship but also ensure that you never get trapped by expectations of perfection.

Pay Attention to How You Feel When Your Spouse or Partner Is not Around

Fortunately, there are several ways you can use to monitor precisely how your relationship is going. These are the three-gauge means of measuring your well-being when trying to figure out how the rest of your life is supposed to be.

The first thing is to ask yourself whether you feel restless or irritable. Do you find yourself dragging through the day after a night of marital bliss? Do you find yourself resenting family and friends even though you are both spending time alone together?

One thing to realize is that love never feeds on tunnel vision. Realize that no matter how you coo like a dove with your partner, if you lack energy, clarity of mind, and benevolence at all times. Yes, you may enjoy all the sex you have together, but if you lack energy the morning or day after, then something is wrong.

So, how can you then know that the other person is "the one?"

When you are first falling in love, know that the person you are about to settle down with is "the one." The last thing you want is to make a mistake, get in the wrong marriage and end up in a lifeless union. Here are some tips that will help you know.

Listen to Your Body And Not Your Mind

Unfortunately, most people choose their mate for reasons that have nothing to do with what they feel and instead have to do with what they think. What is more, we tend to drive our relationships based on how things should be or have been.

This is where you go wrong!

In many cases, you don't lose at love because you allowed your emotions to run away from you, but because you let your mind run away from you.

You may think that you are in love for so many reasons – such as infatuation, lust, status, security, or social acceptance. You think that you have found true love because your current partner meets your expectations and some image you have created in your head of your dream partner. Unless you know how you feel, your choice is only destined to be wrong!

Whenever you imagine your dream partner, the best thing is to transport that form of mental debate to justify your choice so that you can check it with your body. Take in a deep breath, allow your mind and body to relax, and focus by getting out of your head and into your body. What does your gut feeling tell you? Is there a persistent feeling that keeps growing inside, saying that something is wrong? If so, then chances are that your choice is wrong! If you allow your mental image versus physical sensation to lead you, you will never know what you *truly* want.

Notice the Messages From Your Whole Body

When you are in a new relationship, it can be difficult to get clear signals from the rest of your body, because they are likely drowned out by the sexual desires. This explains why you need to pay attention to other important and more subtle feelings – migraines, lack of energy, muscle tension, and stomach pains. These feelings could simply mean that your desires are not really what you need.

However, if you find yourself glowing of love, have liveliness, and a spark of energy, this could be the real deal. If it is only lust or infatuation, chances are that you will feel it in other parts of your life and relationships.

Take a moment to ask yourself the following high emotional intelligence questions:

- Does this relationship energize me and my whole life? Has my work life improved? Am I taking better care of myself?
- Are my head and focus straighter? Am I creative and more responsible?
- Do my "in love feelings" go beyond positive feelings of caring about the other person in the relationship? Am I more generous, more giving and empathic towards the people around me than I was before?

If the responses you get from your body are not exactly what you wanted to hear, it is time to push beyond your fears of loss so that you can look at things from a bigger picture perspective. Finding out at this point that you have not found your true love will spare you of all the heartache, pain, and a pile of negative emotional memories you risk experiencing down the line. Consider this a legacy that can keep you from making the same mistake again and ending up in sour love in the future.

Take a Chance on Reaching Out

When you are in a new relationship, there is often a feeling to be on your guard. We tend to automatically put up barriers and walls when it comes to knowing each other deeply. When you leave yourself open and vulnerable at this point in the relationship, you tend to feel scared, when in the real sense you are trying to find out if the love you feel for the other person is real.

Become the first person to reach out. This is something that will reveal an intimate secret, demonstrate affection, laugh at yourself when everything seems scary. Consider, do the other person's reactions fill you with vitality and warmth? If they do, chances are that you have found a kindred soul. If not, you may have found someone with low emotional intelligence and it is time for you to decide how you wish to respond.

What You Need to Feel Loved vs. What You Want

If you are going to find someone you truly love, then know the difference between what you would like, from what you cannot live without. Here are some exercises that will help you get it right.

Start by selecting at least five features or traits in the other partner you feel are most important to you. Order these character traits in descending order. Some of them may be neat, adventurous, humor, emotional, open, considerate, smart, affectionate, monetarily successful, well-respected, famous, charismatic, spiritual, empowering, nurturing, and conversational, among others.

As you consider each trait, ask yourself if they make you energetic, calm, and emotionally stir you. Find out if these traits make you feel pleasant, unpleasant, or indifferent.

Realize that a desire will be fleeting and superficial, while something you consider a need will automatically register on a deeper level of feelings.

Repeat this exercise over and over again so that you gain a deeper insight into the differences between what you need in love, and what you want. Ask yourself if the other person in the relationship thinks that you are in love to meet these needs.

How to Respond to a Low EQ Partner

One thing to realize is that we don't all grow our emotional muscles at the same rate. If you have a high emotional intelligence compared to your lover, the most important thing is to learn how to respond to them.

What words do you want your partner to hear? Take the time to reconsider what words to use. If you are not sure about what exactly you need and the reasons you need this, there is a high likelihood that your message will be mixed up.

Choose a time when you and your partner are not in a hurry to take a walk together, go on a date, or brunch. While at it, ensure that you are intimately into the conversation so that at the end of it, you both can remember the discussion. During the day, send your partner "I feel" text messages concerning your needs. This will help your partner see what is wrong with them for a chance to improve. For instance, you can text them, "I feel like making love every day, but I don't like the smell of garlic and onions. Would you be willing to brush your teeth before we go to bed?"

There is a high likelihood that partners will respond defensively. If they do, repeat their concerns back to them. Repeat the message and pay attention to what they have to say about it. If possible, keep repeating it over and over again until you are satisfied that they heard what you communicated to them.

Chapter 8:
The Interaction Between EQ and Social Intelligence

It is important to note that social intelligence is about developing experience with people and learning from our failures and successes in our surroundings. In most cases social intelligence is what people commonly refer to as tact, street smartness, or common sense.

What you will note about people with high emotional intelligence is that they carry on conversations with different kinds of people and can verbally communicate with the right words – hence referred to as social expressiveness.

Additionally, such people are adept at learning how to conduct a wide range of social roles and responsibilities. They are well versed on the informal rules of the game, are excellent listeners, and can thoroughly analyze what makes tick the people around them. They know this by focusing their attention on what others have to say and their behaviors.

They not only know various ways of conducting a wide range of social roles but also can put their skills into practice so that they are at ease with a wide range of personalities. In other words, they are careful what impression of themselves they create in other people. This is something that not everyone can do because it needs a delicate balance between controlling and managing your self-image before others and ensuring that you are reasonably authentic in letting others see your true self.

That said, one thing to bear in mind is that social intelligence is more about the future. It came about just so that people could strive to survive and figure out the best way to get along with others, get out of situations, and earn a favorable outcome. It does not matter whether you have paper qualifications in social intelligence. What matters the most is that if you don't know how to apply it in life, you might end up straining or ruining your relationships and lose opportunities.

Yes, there are times when you want to give people feedback so bluntly but choosing your words to convey the message constructively goes a long way in ensuring that you don't end up putting your foot in your mouth. Unlike social intelligence, emotional intelligence is more about the present, hence its close relationship to emotions and feelings. When you read someone's facial expressions, you can easily tell whether they are happy or not. You can tell whether they are nervous, shy, or angry about the situation at hand.

What are some of the social competencies of emotional intelligence?

Read on!

Social Competencies of EQ

Empathy

When we want someone to see things from another's perspective, the first thing we tell them is "*put yourself in their shoes*." That is what empathy is all about. It is the ability to communicate and lead by understanding another person's views, thoughts, and feelings.

When we improve our empathy, we become better versions of ourselves. We strengthen our relationships and make them more meaningful. We strive for success in the workplace. We experience improved health and overall quality of life.

If you look at the top performers in your company, what you will notice is that 90% of them have high emotional intelligence. This is because the more people understand their thoughts, emotions, and feelings, the better they get at understanding someone else's thoughts, emotions, and feelings. When we become better at listening to others, we become better human beings.

But what happens when you lack empathy?

According to research studies, scientists have linked a lack of empathy to a wide range of societal vices – such as theft, murder, and drug dealing among others. Think about the prisoners, are they empathic people? Most likely not. Most of these people lack empathy and didn't care to think about what their victims might have been feeling. If they had empathy, there is a high chance that would have prevented them from committing acts that put them in prison in the first place.

One thing to note is that empathy is connected with the ability to trust other people. When your friends feel that you care, you earn their trust. If they trust you, that simply means that they will be willing to take risks with you and become more open with you. The reason your friends communicate openly with you is that they have built their trust in you.

In other words, as trust continues to grow, it promotes the sharing of information, thoughts, and feelings. It is this form of sharing that expands the foundation upon which you and the others relate with each other. Think about it for a moment: when your friends talk about their interests and ideas, what do you do while you listen to them?

You stop what you are doing to give them your undivided attention. With empathy, you can raise your awareness of other people's feelings during the conversation. When someone asks you for help, it is important that you understand what they are not saying in their words but with their body language.

Bear in mind that a significant portion of communication is often related in non-verbal signals. We may not even realize it, but when we communicate with our facial expressions, noise, gestures, among others, empathy allows us to understand what these non-verbal cues mean. When you master what non-verbal cues mean, you become better at understanding how the other person truly feels.

A solid foundation in emotional intelligence begins with a show of empathy.

You can grow your empathy with practice and the use of the right process. It is possible to take empathy to the next level, something that, in turn, boosts our overall emotional intelligence. When you have the right tools, the process of learning about empathy does not necessarily have to be costly or complicated.

Types of Empathy

There are three types of empathy.

Cognitive Empathy

This refers to the kind of empathy that helps us know what the other person is feeling and what they might be thinking. It is often referred to as "perspective-taking." This type of empathy is connected to the intellect, thought, and understanding. It goes a long way in helping people negotiate, stay motivated, and understand a wide range of perspectives.

The only pitfall to this is not putting yourself in another person's shoes to feel what they are feeling.

One thing to bear in mind is that cognitive empathy is all about thought as much as it is about emotions. Understanding sadness is not the same as feeling sadness.

If you came home upset about losing your job, your partner would respond in this manner. It is the same way a doctor looks at their patients to try and understand their illness. They don't dive into the patient's emotions. In other words, cognitive empathy is about responding to problems with brainpower.

This can be a great asset in situations where you are required to get into the other person's head so that you can interact with their circumstances with tact and understanding. Think of cognitive empathy as mixing apples and oranges. This implies that for you to truly understand what another person is feeling, you have to feel them in some way.

Emotional Empathy

This refers to the ability to feel physically along with another person as though your emotions are contagious. It is concerned with mirroring neurons in the brain, physical sensations, and feelings. It plays a significant role in helping people close their interpersonal relationships and careers.

The pitfalls to this are the fact that emotional empathy can be overwhelming and even inappropriate in some circumstances.

It helps to think of emotional empathy as sound because it involves directly feeling the other person's emotions. Have you heard of the term empath? Well, this means a person with the ability to fully take on the emotional and mental state of another person. Unfortunately, this form of response can seem disconnected from the brain and thinking. However, emotional empathy is deeply rooted in the human mirror neurons.

Each one of us has neurons that fire in certain ways whenever we see someone acting in animal-like behavior. It makes you relate to their actions both in the brain and body. This is exactly what emotional empathy does, feel someone else's experiences in reaction to certain situations.

Think about your loved one for a second. They come to you in tears. What do you feel? You will tend to feel a pull on your heartstrings. When you connect with someone in this way, you strengthen your intimacy and promote a strong bond between the two of you.

Just like cognitive empathy, emotional empathy has its flip-side, and this happens when you cannot manage your distressing emotions. This often leads to emotional burnout. In other words, when you feel too much of what another person is experiencing, you risk experiencing even small interactions as overwhelming.

Compassionate Empathy

This is the kind of empathy in which you not only understand another person's predicament but also feel with them. You are spontaneously touched to help. It is concerned with actions, emotions, and intellect. This plays a significant role in helping you become fully considerate of the other person.

The downside to this kind of empathy is that we are always striving to have it, but we cannot fully have it. In most instances, compassion is necessary. It may be fitting for monetary negotiations, political convincing, among others. It is the first response we give our loved ones, and it strikes a powerful balance between the two parties involved.

It is important to note that the heart and thoughts are not opposing each other. They are intricately connected. It is through compassionate empathy that we honor the natural connection we have with others. When your child comes to you in tears, you are driven to understand why they are crying and want to comfort them by sharing in their emotional experiences and helping them heal. It is a lot to handle.

There are times when we feel going one way or the other with more feelings, thoughts, fixation, and continual changes. The thing about compassionate empathy is that it is about taking the middle ground and then using our emotional intelligence to properly respond to the situation. It is about thinking what the other person might want – to be held, to act to help them fix their situation or just give them a listening ear. You do this without necessarily feeling overwhelmed by sadness or the need to fix things.

In other words, compassion gives us that mindful touch to handle even the toughest of situations.

However, one thing to remember is that empathy is a teeter-totter. In other words, if you go too far into another person's psyche, do you risk losing yours? If you dive too deep in their world, are you risking missing out an integral part of the human experience? If you feel too much, is it inappropriate? If you feel too little, does it hurt?

Understand that not all situations are the same, just like not all the types of empathy are the same.

Take a minute to think about a real-life example in your own life where each type of empathy is applicable. I believe that you have likely found compassionate empathy at some point in your life. Realize that any type of empathy takes practice to gain emotional fitness – just like any other balancing act. Finding a sweet spot where you can empathize effectively is worth the work.

Do it today!

How to Improve Empathy for a Successful Life

- Be quiet inside and out
- Watch as well as listen
- Ask yourself what you are feeling
- Test your instincts
- Challenge yourself
- Get feedback
- Explore the heart and not just your head
- Walk-in other people's shoes and examine your biases
- Cultivate your sense of curiosity

Social Skills

This is a broad term that refers to the skills we need to handle and influence other people's emotions in an effective manner, in the context of emotional intelligence. While this may sound like manipulation, this is as simple as understanding that giving others your smile makes them smile too. Because of your smile, you can make someone feel much better and positive than they were before.

Think of social skills as the last piece of the emotional intelligence puzzle. Once you can understand and manage yourself, only then will you be able to understand other people's emotions and feelings, and influence them.

Some of the most important social skills include:

Communication Skills

This is a vital piece of emotional intelligence. Pay attention to what others have to say and also convey your thoughts and feelings to them in an effective manner.

You may be wondering what makes a good communicator. If you can listen well to people around you, understand what they said, and seek open and full information sharing, then you are likely a good communicator. If you are prepared to hear others' problems and not just ready to only hear good news, then you are a good communicator.

Good communication means dealing with tough situations, setting them straight, and not allowing annoying problems. Ensure that you register and act on emotional signals in communicating so that the message is right.

Leadership Skills

This may sound strange, but one thing to note is that leadership skills are all part of social skills. Emotional intelligence is a huge part of leadership and not vice versa. What to note is that leadership skills and emotional intelligence are inextricably linked to each other. As we have mentioned earlier, people who are tuned into their emotions and those of the people around them have leadership potential.

One of the key aspects of good leadership is influence, and having the ability to bring others along with you. You may refer to this as charisma, but leadership is much deeper than that. In short, it is good emotional intelligence.

To be a good leader you need the ability to articulate a vision and motivate others with it. It does not matter if you are formal or informal; the trick is to ensure that you offer leadership, support, and guide the performance of the people you work with, hold each person accountable, and lead by example.

Persuasion Skills

Persuasion simply refers to the art of motivating people, winning their hearts to your ideas, and leading them on your proposed course of action. If you look around at people you know are persuasive, you will realize that they not only have influence, but also have the ability to read others' emotions in a given circumstance and fine-tune their words so that they appeal to the people around them.

Conflict-management Skills

We all know that conflicts can arise at any given time. They can seem to appear out of thin air. However, the art of resolving conflicts as soon as they arise is crucial both at home and in the workplace. It all begins by raising our awareness to the importance of diplomacy and tact, and how these can be used to address difficulties in various situations.

Being a good conflict manager means that you have to be willing to bring disagreements out in the open when resolving them. Ensure that you use information sharing as a way to encourage debates and open discussions, minimize hidden currents, help each party recognize other's feelings and logical position so that you can obtain a win-win solution.

Chapter 9:
Understanding Emotional Drain and Dealing with Them

Life is not easy; we all know that. There are so many ups and downs, mountains and valleys, highs and lows, and you never really know what to expect. There are times when life is even a little tough for us to handle anything at all. It does not matter what the reason might be, but it finds a way of kicking us when we are down.

One thing we fail to realize is that when we suffer we get emotionally and mentally drained. The thing is that the effects of these shows in ways we can see. Our energy gets sapped to the point that we feel physically exhausted, and all we can do at that point is break down. Know when life is too much so that you can position yourself to better control and manage your emotions. Here are some of the signs to look out for:

Hopelessness

This is a sign that you are emotionally drained. When you have pushed, fought, and clawed through the storms, all your energy gets sapped, and you begin to ask yourself why you are even bothering when things don't seem to get better. This is the point of hopelessness and is dangerous. When you get to this point, you risk making your pain and suffering permanent because you have accepted that this is your way of life. If you are at this point, please seek help.

Crying Often

For most people, crying is something they left behind during their teen years. As we grow older we learn to manage and control our emotions better and we only cry when something big happens in our lives. However, some have been pushed to the limits and crying has become their way of life – a sad movie makes them cry, someone wrongs them and they cry, or an old friend seeks forgiveness from them and they cry.

When you are crying easily like this, it shows you are emotionally exhausted. In other words, even the smallest emotional push brings you into tears.

Insomnia

Are you experiencing trouble getting sleep? This might have something to do with your emotions. When you are emotionally drained you risk suffering from insomnia. You may think that just because you are stressed you will fall asleep easily. However, insomnia occurs often because you are spending most of the time in deep thought, fighting with the demons in your head and have trouble getting a good night's sleep.

Lack of Motivation

When you are emotionally drained, you don't seem to care about striving for anything. You no longer have goals that wake you up in the morning. You are just going through the waves of life, and you let it take you in whatever direction it likes. You find yourself neglecting your work, health, hygiene, and family.

Detachment

If you have been punched hard by life, it is easy to detach yourself from the rest of the people around you. You have allowed the pain to become part of your life and become numb to it, or you have gone through so much that reality no longer clearly exists for you.

Find out what is making you emotionally drained. Is it your partner, family, friends, work, boss? How do you do when someone is sucking your energy reserved dry?

- You think about them all the time
- You are physically exhausted
- You find happiness when they leave

- They don't lift you up
- Once you have been together you feel the need for some downtime
- They demand too much of you
- When they talk they leave you feeling more frustrated than you were before
- You can't seem to say what you mean when you are around them

Things You Can Do if You Are Experiencing Emotional Exhaustion

Exercise

Whenever you are exhausted, exercise is usually the last thing you can think of – after all, working out is a form of physical stress. However, research shows that when we exercise, we relieve mental stress. It will not only help your mental balance, but it will also bring changes to your body, heart, spirit, and metabolism. It offers stimulation and a calming effect against depression and stress.

Research has shown that working out can reduce the levels of body stress hormones like cortisol and adrenaline, and can promote the release of feel-good hormones called endorphins, which are natural painkillers and mood elevators.

Breathing Exercises

Breathing exercises have been shown to help relieve stress and increase relaxation. When someone is panting fast and has a form of erratic breathing, this is an indicator that they are under duress. However, when you take in slow and deep breaths, it has a calming effect. Learn how to control your breathing to mimic relaxation.

The best way to breathe is to do it slowly and deeply while focusing your attention on the movement of your diaphragm – up and down. Then hold your breath for at least seconds before you exhale thinking about relaxation for another five seconds. Repeat this process for about 15-20 times while ensuring that you do it slowly and deeply.

Meditation

Meditation is a practice that has been shown to help relieve stress and calm the mind. This is by lowering both the heart rate and the blood pressure, physiological signs of stress.

The first thing is to choose a place and time when there are no distractions. Get comfortable by finding the right posture that will promote relaxation. Allow your mind to get into a passive mental state and go blank so that thoughts and worries don't get in the way of your relaxation. Watch your thoughts come and go without necessarily passing any judgment.

The trick is to focus your attention on a mental device. You can use simple words of affirmation or mantra so that you repeat them over and over. Alternatively, you can choose to focus your attention on a fixed object within your space. The goal is to ensure that you block out any form of distraction as much as you can. Once you have mastered this, consider dedicating at least 20-30 minutes to meditation every day.

Journaling

If you thought this was just for professional writers, think again. If you ask anyone who has been journaling, they will tell you how much it benefits their mental health by releasing emotional drains.

This is mainly because journaling allows you to write down all your deepest thoughts, emotions, and fears, which is a great way of understanding, managing, and letting go of emotional drains. Research shows that journaling plays a significant role in lowering anxiety, boosting better sleep patterns, improving memory, minimizing depression, and making someone kinder.

One Last Word

Indeed, emotional intelligence is one of the most important things one must have in life to ensure success in every situation.

You probably know people who have mastered the art of managing their emotions. Instead of getting angry when provoked by a stressful situation, they choose to look at the problem from a different perspective to calmly find a solution. These people are excellent decision-makers and have mastered the art of listening to their gut feeling. They have the willingness to look at themselves with an honest eye. They take criticism positively and use it to improve their performance.

I am here to tell you that you can be just like these people. As you begin to accept emotional intelligence into every area of your life, you will begin to see an improvement in your technical abilities, interrelationships, and overall success. It is through emotional intelligence that you can fuel your performance. It impacts your confidence, optimism, self-control, empathy, and social skills, so that you can understand and manage your emotions and accelerate success in every area of your life.

It does not matter what your profession is, whether you work for a small or large organization, whether you are senior or junior in your company. What matters is that realizing how effective you are at controlling your emotional energies is the beginning of a successful adventure. Yes, emotional intelligence may not be something taught and tested in our educational curriculum, but it is really important.

The key to emotional intelligence is to celebrate and reflect on all the positives in your life. No one has a perfect life – we all go through ups and downs. It

I invite you to start working on improving your emotional intelligence and watch how your life changes for the better.

Best of luck!

© **Written by: Joseph Griffith**

Milton Keynes UK
Ingram Content Group UK Ltd.
UKHW022301170823
427026UK00015B/481